CURIOUS PET PALS

MY FRIEND THE BOX TURTLE

Joanne Randolph

WINDMILL
BOOKS
New York

Published in 2011 by Windmill Books, LLC
303 Park Avenue South, Suite # 1280, New York, NY 10010-3657

First Edition

Editor: Jennifer Way
Book Design: Erica Clendening
Layout Design: Julio Gil
Photo Researcher: Brian Garvey

Photo Credits: Cover, pp. 6, 7, 9, 10, 11 (bottom), 12 Shutterstock.com; p. 4 © www.iStockphoto.com/Nancy Brammer; p. 5 Compassionate Eye Foundation/Sam Diephuis; p. 8 © www.iStockphoto.com/Robert Ranson; p. 11 (top) © C. Steimer/age fotostock; p. 13 © Biosphoto/Gunther Michel/Peter Arnold. Inc; pp. 14, 20 © www.iStockphoto.com/Constance McGuire; p. 15 © www.iStockphoto.com/Borut Trdina; p. 16 © www.iStockphoto.com/NoDerog; p. 17 (top) © www.iStockphoto.com/Christine Glade; p. 17 (bottom) © www.iStockphoto.com/Steven Fairbrother; p. 18 © Ed Reschke/ Peter Arnold. Inc; p. 21 Comstock/Getty Images.

Library of Congress Cataloging-in-Publication Data

Randolph, Joanne.
My friend the box turtle / by Joanne Randolph. — 1st ed.
    p. cm. — (Curious pet pals)
Includes index.
ISBN 978-1-60754-979-6 (library binding) — ISBN 978-1-60754-989-5 (pbk.) — ISBN 978-1-60754-990-1 (6-pack)
1. Box turtles as pets—Juvenile literature. I. Title.
SF459.T8R35 2011
639.3'92—dc22
                          2010004893

Manufactured in the United States of America

For more great fiction and nonfiction, go to www.windmillbooks.com

CPSIA Compliance Information: Batch #BW2011WM: For Further Information contact Rosen Publishing, New York, New York at 1-800-237-9932

CONTENTS

MEET THE BOX TURTLE

Have you ever thought about getting a pet turtle? Turtles can make great pets. There are many kinds of turtles.

Box turtles move slowly. Most box turtles move at around .2 miles per hour (.32 km/h).

Painted turtles and diamondback terrapins are two kinds of turtles. Some turtles have funny names, like sliders and cooters.

Box turtles are the most popular pet turtle. Are you thinking about getting a pet turtle? This book will tell you more about box turtles and how to care for them.

Box turtles are kept as pets, but they also live in the wild. There are many different kinds of box turtles.

Box turtles generally grow to about 8 inches (20.3 cm) long. T[he] males have dark red or orange eye[s]

Some of these include eastern, western, desert, Florida, Gulf Coast, and ornate box turtles.

Box turtles can be shy. This eastern box turtle has closed itself into its shell. It is hard for animals that want to eat the box turtle to get it out of its shell.

Box turtles are small to medium-sized turtles. Like other turtles, they can pull their head and legs into their shells if they think they are in danger. Then they can close up their shell to stay safe!

7

In the wild, box turtles live in lots of different **habitats**. You might see them in swampy forests or grass-covered fields. Some kinds of box turtles even live in the desert.

Box turtles can be found in grassy places like this one. Most box turtles live in forests and only come out into grassy places for a short time, though.

All box turtles like a **humid**, or wet, habitat best. Even desert turtles will dig down into the soil to find moist earth.

The colors of this box turtle's shell blend in with its surroundings. This helps the turtle hide from animals that hunt it.

Wild box turtles should be treated with **respect**. Never take a box turtle from the wild to keep as a pet!

HOME SWEET HOME

How can you make a good home for a pet box turtle?

Once your turtle is used to you, you can pick it up and hold it. You can bring it inside or outside as long as you keep an eye on it!

Turtle owners have found that glass tanks and aquariums are not the best turtle homes. Instead, a large plastic tub is the best for turtles.

Turtles are **reptiles**. Reptiles cannot make their own heat. You need to make sure they have a place to warm their bodies. For this job, you will need special heating pads and heating lamps.

A pet turtle's home needs to have a few different areas to be comfortable for the animal.

There should be a dry part that has potting soil mixed with bark. You can use a spray bottle to **mist** this mixture and keep it moist.

This turtle pen is filled with soil, bark, and straw. A good pen will also have a pool and places for the turtles to hide.

A turtle also needs places to hide and to sleep in its home. A wooden or cardboard box works well for this. The box should have straw or more of the soil mix, so your turtle can burrow into its "bed."

Your turtle will be happy if there is a pool in its habitat. The turtle needs to be able to get in and out easily, though. A low pan or dish can make a good pool.

Box turtles are land turtles. They do like to swim and they like their home to be wet, even if they are not in the water most of the time.

The water in the pool needs to be kept clean. This means you need to change its water every day. Doing this will keep your pet healthy and happy for a long time.

CARING FOR YOUR TURTLE

Box turtles need to be misted with water at least once a day.

Check your turtle often to make sure it is healthy. The eyes, mouth, and shell should look clean and clear.

A spray bottle is an easy way to do this. Spraying water over the turtle habitat keeps the air humid. This is important for your box turtle.

16

Misting the turtle's habitat with a spray bottle will keep your pet healthy and happy.

Turtles that get too dry can have health problems. These can include eye problems and breathing problems. It is also important to find a vet, or pet doctor, who knows how to take care of turtles.

Box turtles are **omnivores**. This means they eat both plants and animals. Be sure to feed your box turtle lots of different foods.

If you keep your box turtle outside, you can grow yummy foods in its pen. The turtle will enjoy eating these fresh foods.

They can eat worms, slugs, fruits, berries, mushrooms, and turtle food from a pet store. This will keep them healthy and happy.

Box turtles like to eat small animals like slugs.

Turtles need calcium to keep their shells healthy. You can buy vitamins at the pet store that will give your turtle the calcium and other nutrients it needs.

It is not a good idea to keep wild box turtles as pets. The number of box turtles in the wild is falling fast because homes and roads are being built in their habitats.

Some pet stores sell turtles caught in the wild. Do not add to the problem by getting your turtle from one of these places.

If you would like to get a pet box turtle, look for a turtle **breeder**. Once you get your box turtle, take good care of it. This way you can enjoy your new pet for a long time!

GUESS WHAT?

Box turtles can eat the kinds of mushrooms that would make people sick or could even kill them.

Female box turtles generally lay from 2 to 4 eggs in their nests. This group of eggs is called a clutch.

A turtle's shell is covered in scales called scutes. A box turtle's shell has 38 scutes on its top shell and 12 on the bottom shell.

Box turtles are the only turtles that can pull their bodies completely inside their shells and close them.

Box turtles often live until they are about 30 years old. Some box turtles have even lived until they were 50 years old!

GLOSSARY

BREEDER (BREE-der) A person who brings a male and a female together so they will have babies.

HABITAT (HA-beh-tat) The surroundings where an animal or a plant naturally lives.

HUMID (HYOO-med) Damp or moist.

MIST (MIST) Covering with fine droplets of water or other wet matter.

OMNIVORES (OM-nih-vorz) Animals that eat both plants and animals.

REPTILES (REP-tylz) Cold-blooded animals with thin, dry pieces of skin called scales.

RESPECT (rih-SPEKT) To think highly of someone or something.

READ MORE

Stone, Lynn M. *Box Turtles*. Minneapolis, MN: Lerner Publications, 2007.

Bartlett, Richard D. and Patricia Bartlett. *Box Turtles: Facts & Advice on Care and Breeding*. New York: Barron's Educational Series, 2001.

Gibbons, Whit, and Judy Greene. *Turtles: The Animal Answer Guide.* Baltimore, MD: The Johns Hopkins University Press, 2009.

INDEX

WEB SITES

For Web resources related to the subject of this book, go to: www.windmillbooks.com/weblinks and select this book's title.